D0556974

This book is dedicated to Linda who works more magic with less resources than any person I know. She's the person I respect most in the world and the best friend a girl could ever have.

Contents

Forward

When facing hard times, the pressures of trying to make ends meet day in and day out can be truly daunting. The stress of constant worry is what defeats us more often than not. "How will we pay the light bill?" "Is my employer going to fire me?" "Will we lose the house?" It can be as devastating to your overall well-being as the economy is to your wallet.

When you're going through hard times it helps to know you are not alone. You may be new to the world of paycheck-to-paycheck, broke-ass living but it's a very big community. It's populated with every kind of ethnicity, nationality, religion and class. How we get through is with a little help from our friends and that's what this book is about. How we make great family dinners work with little to nothing is what I am going to attempt to teach you. I do not claim they are gourmet nor are they always the healthiest, but there are tricks to that as well, these recipes are time tested and will feed a family of 4 for pennies a day.

This book for the most part will cover entrees. You'll want to accompany the recipe with your favorite sides of veggies and salads. You'll also notice that these recipes are very basic and simple to create. The reason for this is very simple, if you're struggling and trying to stretch your food dollar, it doesn't make sense to offer you a recipe with a lot of ingredients and seasonings that you don't have on hand or can't afford to procure. Also, I wanted to leave room for your own creativity. Find out what you like. Add or subtract as you desire. No recipe should be set in stone; where's the fun in that? Another reason for keeping these recipes as simple as they are is time. If you're a struggling single parent, the idea of cooking a meal after a long day at the office can hardly be appealing. The majority of the recipes contained can be cooked in 20 minutes. When your children are hungry and ready for dinner and your boss asks you to stay late at work, a twenty minute dinner is infinitely more do-able than a more elaborate meal.

I learned these tricks growing up in a single parent house in the seventies with a mother who struggled to feed two kids working as a secretary. I have never had money and was born with the broke-ass gene so I feel uniquely qualified to advise on how make a meal out of next to nothing. With some careful planning and a cabinet full of basic low-cost staples, you can make it work. So what are we waiting for? Let's start with the basics:

The Broke-Ass Basics

The following are items you should stock in your cabinet and fridge. They are reasonably inexpensive and when used wisely can keep you out of the grocery store. For the most part, you probably already have most of these items on the lists in your home already. These aren't exotic, never heard of it, ingredients. If you're struggling, it's pretty difficult to go shopping for a lot of new stuff. Take it a bit at a time. Most of the recipes only require three or four items from the shopping lists. Stock up on what you can and like, leave the rest for another day. This is supposed to be stress-free.

When you go shopping for your staples, choose the store wisely. Aldi is pretty good for most everything on the list. Personally, I do not care for Aldi and shop at Wal-Mart, but that's just a personal choice. You can save tremendous amounts just by changing stores. The price differences can be quite shocking. I'm not a coupon clipper and typically go for the generic brand simply because in processed food I've never experienced a truly noticeable difference between generic and name brand. However, this might not be your experience. I've based the recipes on truly cheap, generic ingredients so your experience with the recipes will be the same if you go the same route.

Modify these lists as you wish, I for instance no longer eat cow, so I substitute ground turkey or chicken. These are great options for you as well as they are considerably cheaper per pound than cow meat. They are also a somewhat healthier option than red meat. You can modify the list however you think suits you. Most of the recipes are quite flexible, fun to make and most importantly, taste great. You may not have the coin for caviar, but that doesn't mean you have to eat food without flavor.

Shopping Lists (if you don't already have them)

Dry/Canned Goods

Chicken Stock (preferably dry but not the bullion)

Big cans (28 oz) Crushed tomatoes

Diced tomatoes

Canned vegetables all varieties and lots of them

Tomato paste can if necessary but the tube variety is a better value

Dry package gravies any variety

Cream of mushroom soup

Pork & Beans big cans or lots of normal size

Spaghetti

Egg Noodles

Macaroni & Cheese

Pinto Beans

Rice (I do brown but your preference)

Canned enchilada sauce

Flour

Sugar (I do Wal-Mart version of Splenda again your preference)

Canned Kidney Beans

Canned tuna

Canned salmon

Campbell's Golden Mushroom soup (this is a splurge if you can find it but well worth it)

Perishables

3 lb Bag of boneless skinless chicken breasts

Cheap hot dogs (not the good all beef, get the chicken, pork mix)

Whole chicken (if affordable, go for roaster if you can, fryer if not)

Tube of ground beef (get a 5lb tube, I'll show you how to make it last forever)

Cheese shreds Mexican mix

10 lb bag of potatoes

Light Soy Milk (Just trust me on this one, cheaper than cow and you're not a baby cow)

Aldi or Wal-Mart brand butter (margarine in a pinch but some things you just don't skimp on....much)

Tube of breakfast or Italian sausage

Corn tortillas

Savoy cabbage or regular cabbage (Savoy's just easier to work with)

Green peppers (buy by the pound not each. Each is a rip off)

Bag of romaine hearts (3 to a bag)

Bag of baby spinach

Green onions or scallions

Shallots (not critical but oh so good)

Celery bunch

Optional:

1 lb Ground turkey tubes

1 lb Ground chicken tubes

Spices

Garlic salt ($.50 at Wal-Mart or Dollar Store), pepper, chili powder, bread crumbs Italian flavor is nice this is optional but very helpful, adobo also optional, liquid smoke

How to make a pound of ground round make 4 meals

As previously mentioned my mother fed herself, my sister and me on a secretary's salary. If you think the pay for a secretary is bad now, imagine it forty years ago. One way she did it was to get 3 lbs of ground beef and have me take out an old mail weight scale and measure out the ground beef into ¼ servings. I'd wrap each quarter pound serving in aluminum foil and throw them in the freezer. Each dinner I'd take out one of the packages to include in one of the meals. Now right now you're thinking she starved us but once you stop to think about it and when you see how the meat is used in the recipes, you'll see just how genius this is. We had more than enough for the three of us and leftovers to boot.

You see when you use ground meat, unless it's in a hamburger or meatball, you're not getting a whole lot. When you brown the meat and add it to a dish, you cannot tell a pound from a quarter. The same applies if you're using ground turkey or chicken, by the way. You can't easily buy more than one pound of those meats generally but you can still quarter them the same. You'll find it's an even better savings on average than ground beef.

Go ahead and try it for yourself. If you really feel like it's not enough, you can certainly defrost more than one. But when you try these recipes, try it with the ¼ lb. If it doesn't work just add in additional meat.

If you don't have a scale, just guesstimate it. If you have 1lb of meat you should have 4 equal sections, 5lbs= 20, 3lbs= 12, etc. To this day I can still get a quarter pound of meat and wrap it without weighing. Give it a shot.

Whatever happened to starting a meal with Soup?

When I was a kid and we went out to eat, the waiter always asked if we'd like soup or salad, sometimes you'd get both. It's still around but not much. If you do get it, they bring you a little teaspoon of chicken broth and not 5 minutes later they show up with your entrée. It's really designed to turn the table over quickly. The sooner they get you in and out, the sooner they can get another customer in. To be honest, when I was waitressing, one of my goals was to get them in and out in a hurry. There's nothing worse for a server than someone sitting there all night. That being said, I can't help thinking that an important part of the meal is missing.

I find that if I start a meal off with a soup or salad, I eat far less than I would without it. Usually by the time I get home from work, I'm famished and eat something I really shouldn't and too much of it. When I have a nice bowl of soup, I calm down, my blood sugar is steady and I don't stuff my face. Now when you're squeezing the life out of every penny, soup, which is generally easy and cheap to make, can be a great starter. Sometimes, a bowl of soup is all I really need in the evenings. Sometimes I need a bit more but not much. So let's get started with soup.

Best Veggie Soup

Okay, there's a lot of variation available with this soup. Feel free to experiment. Add noodles or rice anything you like. I sometimes like to start the base by sautéing some onions in olive oil then building the additional flavors. Get creative with it and have fun. Here's the basic quick cook recipe.

¼ c Chicken Soup base

1 can crushed tomatoes

1 can each of your favorite vegetables

1 tbsp tomato paste

Approx. 1 qt of water

Begin this one simply by getting out your stock or pasta pot. Add two cups of water and chicken soup base. Heat and stir soup base is dissolved and aromatic. Add another cup of water. Begin to add each of the canned vegetables. Make sure to drain the water from each can. If you're using cut corn, do not drain the water from this can, include it in the soup. Let this heat to a simmer and let it simmer for a while, maybe 10 minutes. Now add the <u>crushed</u> tomatoes. Once that's incorporated add the tomato paste and stir till combined. Soup's on!

One note: If you can afford it, add some fresh diced zucchini. It's truly delightful.

Family Friendly Dinners

Chuck Wagon!

Your kids are going to love this. You may not think it's all that, but it's a great kid friendly meal and a perfect example of how you can use less meat and still feed an army. If you're a big kid like me, you'll love it as much as the little ones.

¼ ground beef (turkey or chicken)

1-2 large cans (or 4 smaller cans) of Pork & beans

¼ cup of sugar (or Splenda)

Brown your ground beef, add a pinch or two of garlic salt to taste. Once brown, drain about half the fat into a container, preferably a repurposed coffee can. Set the pan to one side.

In a large stock or pasta pot, empty the cans of Pork & Beans into it and place over a medium heat and let simmer.

Add the meat and fat from the pan to the pork & beans and incorporate.

Once the mixture is fully heated and simmering add the sugar and stir until dissolved then serve.

Note: I really encourage you to use a sugar substitute for this recipe. The recipe must have the sweetener but it doesn't have to have quite so many calories.

Sis' Favorite

I really debated on adding this recipe to the book. It's is so crazy simple that I thought I shouldn't bother. But then I considered that if this book is about anything, it's about making a meal when you have nothing to make it with. I cannot tell you how many times I have had to come up with something for dinner and stood in front of an open, empty fridge and thought, "no way". If you've ever had to come up with a meal when your fridge was practically empty and your bank account even emptier, I would wager you'd welcome an idea or two. That's how this recipe started life. One day it was time for dinner and there was nothing to make it with. The story goes like this:

One day it was time for dinner and there was absolutely nothing in the refrigerator besides a package of hot dogs. We never bought hot dog buns unless it was a special occasion. If you wanted a hot dog on a bun, you got a piece of bread and wrapped it around a hot dog. That might have been an option on this day but we didn't have any bread. After staring at the package of hot dogs for what seemed like hours, I thought, "What about hot dogs and beans?" Great, if we'd had a can of pork and beans, which we didn't. Moving on to the pantry, I found only spaghetti and tomato sauce. Thus was born my sister's all-time favorite meal, hot dogs and spaghetti.

It probably seems bizarre to you, but she was only 7 years old and that's what 7 year olds like. I liked it as well and so did my mother, though probably not as much as my sister did. It's a real kid-pleaser kind of recipe and amazingly fast to prepare. The truth is, every now and again I still get a craving for it. Told you I was a big kid.

Actually it is a fun alternative to traditional spaghetti Bolognese or spaghetti & meatballs. I suggest getting the cheap hot dogs because they actually taste better in this dish than the good all beef hot dogs. And truth be told, there are few things you can do with the chicken/pork mix hot dogs. They simply have to be used in a recipe like this because they are not good on their own.

Hot dogs and spaghetti

1 lb spaghetti

½ package of cheap hot dogs

1 28oz can of crushed tomatoes

Can't get simpler than those ingredients, can you? Preparation is even easier; get your pasta pot out and fill with about a quart of water. Add a tablespoon of chicken soup base to the water. (It gives a nice taste to your pasta) Cook the pasta as recommended. When pasta is done, drain the water into a container and store for later use. (We waste nothing in Broke-ass land.) Slice the hot dogs into ¼ inch pieces. Add the hot dogs to the pasta. Add the crushed tomatoes and serve. How simple is that?

You might be saying, but wait, you didn't cook the hot dogs! You didn't cook the crushed tomatoes! The hot dogs are already cooked. You actually just heat hot dogs not cook them and the heat from the pasta warms the bite size pieces perfectly along with the crushed tomato sauce. If you like, you can slice the hot dogs while the pasta is cooking and add them in the water. They should plump nicely, but be careful to only do this for a few minutes tops. The reason why we don't pre-heat the cheap hot dogs is because they become very rubbery and lose what flavor they have.

My Favorite

I think I love rich and creamy dishes most because while the ingredients may be simple, you feel satisfied and nourished. It's comfort food, let's face it. This is still one of my go-to meals when I'm feeling like I need a little lovin'.

Tuna Noodle Minus the Casserole

½ package of egg noodles

1 can of tuna

1 can cream of mushroom soup

Cook the pasta according to package directions, remember to add a tablespoon of chicken broth to the water. When done, drain the water into a container and store for later use.

Add the can of tuna drained. Many of you prefer the package tuna as do I, but unfortunately the can tuna is much cheaper which is why I include it in the shopping list. If you just can't go for canned tuna, use two of the packaged or one large size packaged tuna.

Add the cream of mushroom soup to the pasta and tuna stirring to combine then serve.

Again, I'm not cooking the cream of mushroom soup beforehand. It's truly not necessary to heat the soup before adding to the hot pasta but if you feel like it should be heated you can add the soup to a microwave bowl and heat for about a minute or two in the microwave. But seriously, save yourself the dishwashing and just add it to the pasta.

Cheap & Easy Cheater Chili

To do chili properly, you need to make your own chili powder from actual chilies and make a paste and chop the meat and cook it in the oven and..., UGH! Who has that kind of time? Well I did it once and maybe one day I'll do it again but I'll have to take a vacation day to do it. Real chili is fantastic, but honestly, I like my near-chili much better. It's also much, MUCH, easier to make and can be made in a hurry.

1 yellow onion (you can leave out, but why?)

1 package (1/4 lb) Ground beef or chicken or turkey

1 can 28oz Crushed tomatoes or Diced

1-2 cans of dark red kidney beans

½ bell pepper whatever color you desire

Chili powder and garlic salt

Take a tablespoon of oil, preferably olive but whatever oil you have on hand is fine (more on oils later). Heat the oil in a pasta pot over a low heat. Peel and chop the onion finely. Add to the oil and sauté till the onion is translucent. It's important you keep the heat low during this process so you don't overcook the onion. They shouldn't go brown. While the onion is cooking, chop the bell pepper into finely cut pieces about an eighth of an inch cubed. Don't worry much about the measurement though. It should be just small enough so you don't get a huge chunk on your spoon. Add the pepper to the onion and sauté just until the onion is see-through. Add the ground meat and brown. While browning the meat, season it with some garlic salt. Once the meat is brown, add in the chili powder. Ready-made chili powder is pretty much useless unless you use a ton, which I'm not suggesting, but you'll need to put enough in to give it a chili taste so add a little at this point but hold off on adding more until we add the tomatoes so you'll know what tastes good to you.

Next add your beans. Now a word about the beans; I choose dark red because of their nutrition value as well as the value to your pocketbook, but there are other beans that taste better in the chili. Navy beans or chili beans may taste better to you, so experiment with it since there are no hard and fast rules on this mock-chili.

Now add your tomatoes, you can used crushed tomatoes or diced tomatoes or both, if you choose to use both, get the smaller cans of both or perhaps use the large can of crushed with a smaller can of diced.

Finally, at this point you want taste the chili and determine if you want to add more chili powder. At this point the chili's ready to serve. Enjoy.

Let's talk about oil baby!

Fair warning, the following may disgust you and cause you nightmares. Only dare to read on and you may be pleasantly surprised.

In my home growing up we saved grease. There, I've said it publically and without shame. In fact in most homes in my neighborhood, they saved grease. I was actually shocked when I grew older and discovered that most people found this distasteful.

The practice came from the depression-WWII era when people couldn't afford Crisco and later oil products were rationed so homemakers saved the oil from cooking bacon and other meat products to be reused for other dishes.

My Father was born in 1927 and my mother in 1942 so they grew up with the practice and continued it in our home. I actually didn't know you could buy Crisco in the store until I was in my late teens. It's funny, we had an old Crisco can in which we kept the repurposed oil and referred to the name whenever we were going to cook with it but I suppose I just thought we purchased the can to put the oil in. More than likely, the can was used at some point and we just refilled it with the used oil.

Other families had a coffee can they used to keep it the oil in and some had mason jars of it. I actually use a mason jar myself, but to be honest I don't have a really good used oil stash. The thing that makes used oil so good is the combination of flavors you get. The oil from the bacon, fried chicken, pork chops, & hamburgers you cook all combine to make whatever you're cooking next in the oil taste absolutely amazing. I rarely if ever eat any of those dishes so I don't have a lot of oil to add to the mix. My stash is ok, but some folks have an amazing stash.

As mentioned you might think this practice is gross and you're probably right. I think of it more as seasoning than anything else and frankly the cost of oil is pretty outrageous so you might want to try an open mind on this one. I would also suggest you consider that the fast food chains we all frequent use the same oil day after day. They change it once a week or less frequently depending on the requirements of the municipality they are in. Quite often they cook everything from fries to fish in the same oil so it's not as unusual as you might think.

A few things stand out in my memory of great dishes made with the used oil. Greens in particular, one of my favorite things in the world to eat, are not complete without a smidge of used oil in the water. Another is my mother's steak fries. OMG folks, best fries ever.

Best Fries Ever

This is the way my mother made them. You can make them with Crisco or whatever oil you choose and they are quite good, but the best way is with the used oil

2-3 Russet potatoes (new potatoes are good and closer to the original taste if frying in "new" oil)

1 cup of used oil

Get out your skillet pan and add the cup of oil and heat on low. Peel and slice the russets to steak fries size.

Add them to the pan immediately and cook slow. One of the keys to her technique was that it took a little while for the fries to cook.

To be honest, I'm not sure when this idea that fries should be crispy came about. Fries should be greasy and almost creamy texture. It's not good for you but if you wanted good for you, you'd eat a salad. When I was a kid, fries were always bendable and if you squeezed them you'd get grease. Now the ones you get from that fast food joint with supposedly the "best fries" could cut your throat with how sharp and crispy they are. They're fine, but there's a place for greasy totally bad for you fries in everyone's life if you ask me.

Easy Chili Mac

It may seem odd to you, but I didn't know people ate macaroni & cheese as a main dish or entrée until I was at least 13. In my house mac & cheese was always a side dish until one day I was fishing around for a new idea for dinner when we had next to nothing in the pantry besides mac & cheese. Now I still wouldn't serve mac & cheese as a dinner entrée but I did think, well what if we make it into chili mac? That's how I invented easy chili mac. You'll make the macaroni & cheese according to package instructions with a couple of exceptions, instead of cow milk, I want you to use the soy milk. Soy milk is better tasting and better for you. If you don't believe me, try it in your coffee and cereal. You'll truly love it. The other exception is the butter. For this recipe in particular you can use margarine. Margarine is terrible and butter is amazing but for this recipe it doesn't matter. You need a little fat to make the mac & cheese and the margarine will do just fine for this and save you a few bucks.

Easy Chili Mac Ingredients

1 box macaroni & cheese (any kind will do, generic is perfect)

1 package (1/4 lb) ground beef, chicken or turkey

1 can 28 oz crushed tomatoes

As mentioned, begin by preparing the mac & cheese according to package directions with the two exceptions previously mentioned, milk and margarine.

While the water is boiling for the mac & cheese, brown the ground meat in a skillet and season with garlic salt and a little chili powder. Once brown, add the crushed tomatoes and simmer on a very low heat while you are completing the preparation of the macaroni & cheese. Once the mac & cheese is complete, add the ground meat & crushed tomato mixture to the mac & cheese. Stir to combine and serve.

Couple of notes: You may have noticed I did not suggest you drain the ground beef. It is always better to drain ground beef but it I'm not sure you should waste it. Unless you produce a tremendous amount of fat, I'd leave it in. It adds a lot of flavor to your food. Most decent ground meat has very little fat now anyway you may not get enough to drain. Since I use turkey, I never have enough to drain. You may drain the meat as you wish. If you do decide to, drain about half of it into your "save the grease" can.

That's a Tasty Meatball!

Meatballs are a real treat if done properly. I'm going to share with you my best meatball recipe. Prepare this on a weekend evening when you're just sitting around watching TV. You can freeze them or refrigerate them for later use in our recipes. The reason why is that meatballs are not a weekday kind of recipe. They take more time than most of the other recipes in this book and it's kind of pain to do when you're running around shuffling kids. It takes a little work but so incredibly worth the effort.

1 package (1/4 lb) ground meat (beef, chicken or turkey)

1 package of tube sausage (whatever kind, Italian sausage or breakfast)

¼ cup of Italian bread crumbs

¼ cup of soy milk

Chicken water from pasta you've been saving

Garlic salt & pepper to taste

First thing, pour the chicken broth water into a nice 2 qt pot and heat on low. What you're aiming for with the water is just a low simmer. It should not be a rolling boil. If it becomes a rolling boil turn the heat down.

In a large bowl, mix the ground meat and sausage together to incorporate. Add the bread crumbs, milk, garlic salt and pepper and mix well. This is my least favorite part of the job because I don't like my hands getting dirty. If you feel the same, get the kids they love it.

Now time to make your meatballs. Just take a pinch of meat. You don't need or want them to be huge. It should be about the size of a quarter in diameter. To make the meatball round, you toss from one hand to the other. It's not a big gesture, you're not pitching for the Yankees. This is just a casual toss from hand to hand. I few tosses back and forth will get the round shape you need. This is much better the rolling technique which doesn't work because most of the meat stays on your hands.

Once you get about 10 meatballs, start adding them to your water. You'll notice they sink to the bottom or kind of bounce in the water. Once they start to float, they are done. Should take literally 4-5 minutes tops. Once they do start to float, take them out and put them in a baking dish. Let the water reheat again, while it is, you can be getting the next batch ready for the water. Done right, you should get about 30-40 meatballs. This is an excellent recipe to do with kids, by the way. They love making them and they can get a little bonding time with daddy or mommy.

Take the baking dish with the completed meatball and place it in a 350 degree oven for about 10 minutes. This gives it a nice brown crust or shell. Now take them out let them cool about 5 minutes. Steal a couple, then put them away for the later serving.

A little tale about pasta sauce

When I was a kid they came out with Ragu. We never had Ragu in our house. I'm reminded of this one-woman show Julia Sweeney did called, "God Said Ha". In it she talks about how if she mentioned pasta marinara to her parents, her mother would look confused and say, "you mean the noodles with the red topping?" It was kind of like that in my house. "Marinara, what the heck is that?" But when Ragu came out and I had it for the first time, OMG! That stuff was the bomb! I was crazy for it. I told my mother, "we've got to get some Ragu!" her reply was short and to the point, "No". Oh, I was so ill-treated. Meanwhile I'd mooch off my friends when they had spaghetti for dinner, all because my mean old mommy deprived me of it. Our "marinara" was tomato sauce. My mother didn't feel it needed to be any fancier than that and we really couldn't afford it. I joke about it, but things were really that bad. Ragu was a $1.59 then and tomato sauce was $.35.

Now that I'm older, I've taken a really good look at Ragu, I'm a pretty good cook and can make a mean marinara, but I hadn't used Ragu since my late teens simply because my tastes had sophisticated enough that Ragu just doesn't do it for me anymore. But I began to wonder what was it about Ragu and the other "pasta sauces" that turned me on so? Sugar.

Duh? I had no idea till I looked at the ingredients.
Naturally I craved it, I was a kid and it was sweet.

It seems strange to me now that anyone would think to
put sugar or corn syrup in a pasta sauce, but of course
they put it in just about everything. The strange thing I
realize now is our tomato sauce was SO much better.
Really I cannot imagine some of the recipes in this book
with a pasta sauce. It would just ruin it. Now today I
don't use tomato SAUCE, I use crushed and diced
tomatoes. It's somewhat less processed and less sugar,
also you get more tomato flavor. I think a marinara
should be pretty simple and straightforward.

If you decide to try some of the marinara pasta recipes,
be sure to use either crushed (preferred) or diced.
Please don't use a pasta sauce, it's not the same. You
may swear by Ragu and just to be clear I still like Ragu
& Prego or any of the other pasta sauces, but I just now
realize how much value it really has and I think my
mom was right.

Marinara Sauce

Spaghetti marinara is pretty much a given on a tight
budget, but I'm sharing my marinara recipe because it
is simple and versatile. You can use this as plain
marinara, add meat for a Bolognese or add the
yummy meatballs. You get spaghetti 3 different ways
with one sauce. Make it ahead of time and store in the

fridge for easy access. Easy is my middle name, oh, uh, wait that came out wrong.

1 28oz can of crushed tomatoes

1 small onion

2 garlic cloves

1 tbsp olive oil (olive is best here but whatever oil you have is fine in a pinch)

Fresh basil if you have it is also nice in this recipe but not required

In a large skillet heat the oil on a low heat. Low and slow is the way to go. No one likes a burned tomato sauce. When you see little wisps of smoke from the oil in the pan, oil is ready. But before it gets ready, mince your garlic.

Best way to mince garlic:

Take the flat side of a large butcher knife, lay it against the peeled garlic clove, with the base of the palm of your hand, strike the knife crushing the garlic. Then take the same knife and chop the garlic very finely. Those mincers are nice but you waste too much. This is the best way believe me.

Add the garlic to the now heated oil, keeping the heat very low, sauté the garlic until aromatic. Next chop the onion. The onion should be chopped as fine as the garlic or as fine as you can get it. You want the flavor of the onion, not a big chunk of onion. Add it to the pan. Sauté until the onion and garlic almost disappear in the pan. Now add your tomatoes. If you like it a little chunky add a small can of diced tomatoes. Simmer for about 10 mins. Store it until ready to serve with pasta.

For the Bolognese, take a ground meat package and brown in a skillet. Next add to the sauce and simmer for 5 minutes until fully heated. You may also want to try a little bit of sausage in your Bolognese. It does give your sauce a nice kick of flavor. Brown the sausage with the ground meat and add to your marinara. Serve with pasta.

Golden Mushroom Pasta w/Meatballs

In case you thought the meatballs you made were just for spaghetti, I'm sharing this yummy weeknight meal which is going to be one of your favorites. Campbell's Golden Mushroom soup is the key to this recipe. It's a little pricey, but it can stretch a long way with a half a cup of water mixed in. Use a half a cup of the chicken water you've been saving to keep the flavor.

½ package of egg noodles

1 can Campbell's Golden Mushroom Soup

15-20 meatballs

Cook the egg noodles according to the package in water with a tablespoon of chicken soup base. Remember to save the water you drain from the pot.

Add the meatballs to the noodles. If they were frozen, heat them up again in the microwave.

Add the golden mushroom soup and ½ a can of the chicken water to egg noodles. Stir to combine and serve. Mmmmmm wait till you taste it.

As a variation on this recipe, take all the same steps but use different gravy flavors and use ground meat instead of the meatballs.

Red Beans & Rice

I love anything healthy that tastes great and is a comfort food too. You can't beat beans and rice for healthy and satisfying. The trick to red beans is soaking overnight. Don't want to soak? Don't cook the beans. It's just not going to come out the same if you don't soak them. I've tried, believe me, but it always comes out wrong. You want a creamy texture to the beans. I make this a bit healthier with brown rice instead of white, but I won't lie to you and tell you it's just as good. White rice and red beans tastes much better but I don't mind the rice difference if the beans are well done.

1 package of pinto beans

1 bay leaf (cuts the gas from the beans)

1 ham hock (optional, sort of)

1 tbsp of liquid smoke

Soak the beans in a pot of water overnight with the bay leaf. Add a little chicken soup base to the water.

Next day drain the water (do not save this water), refill it and put it on a medium heat add a spoonful of your used grease. Also, add the liquid smoke, it is really vital to the flavor of the dish. Let the beans cook about 90 mins adding water as necessary.

Cook the rice with a bit of chicken soup base in the water. This helps brown rice tremendously.

Serve the beans with the rice.

Note that I deliberately left out the ham hock. The ham hock is just gross to me but I understand that without it you just don't get the proper flavor of the beans. It also seems a little wasteful. I've never known anyone to eat it and it's just in there for the flavor. Still I'll add them and then once the beans are done give the ham hock to the dogs as a treat. You can decide how you feel about them they are relatively cheap so consider it.

The Magical Bag of Chicken Breasts

Chicken breast can be completely ridiculous in price when purchased boneless and skinless. But if you're anything like me, you want it fast and convenient. While I can debone a chicken P.D.Q. I don't want to do it. Hooray for the bag o' chicken breasts, my lifesaver. It's not very expensive and the chicken breasts, while not exactly top quality, are certainly wonderful in various recipes. If used wisely you can make just a few of these chicken breasts stretch into several different meals.

Preparing the chicken breasts:

Take out 4 chicken breasts and place in a baking dish. Take out a salad dressing, oil based like Italian or vinaigrette (Italian is best). Should be a light version but whatever you have will do. Baste the chicken breasts with the salad dressing. Sprinkle a little garlic salt on the chicken breasts and bake in a 350 degree oven for about 20-25 minutes. They should not be overcooked. If it starts to look dry, take them out. These do not take long to cook so watch them carefully. You should have quite a bit of juice run off, drain this and store it for other recipes. Set the breasts aside to cool.

Once cool, hand shred the chicken breasts. No food processors allowed, I'm afraid, you want long strands of meat. This is not a truly laborious process but I could

think of several things I'd rather be doing. Still it's
worth the work and you can do it while watching tv.

Now that you've gotten them shredded separate the
meat into 3 more or less equal parts and store in
containers until ready to use. Now that you've got
them, what do you do with them? The following
recipes use a portion of shredded chicken each.

Chicken Salad

Chicken salad is very versatile and yummy dish. You can use it on top of a bed of romaine and/or spinach or you could make about four sandwiches. Here's my recipe for chicken salad but play with it and make it your own.

1 portion shredded chicken

¼ cup light Ranch dressing

1 stalk of celery

2-3 scallions or green onion

½ bell pepper

10-15 grapes (approximate, please don't count out the grapes a handful will do)

1/8 c Raisins

1/8 c Craisins

1 small apple diced (whatever in season)

Add one portion of shredded chicken to a bowl. Add ¼ cup of light ranch dressing, add veggies celery, bell pepper & green onion. Add fruit, grapes, raisins, craisins and diced apple. Mix to incorporate all chill for about 20 minutes then serve.

Note: You should use whatever fruits & veggies you have on hand. There are no hard and fast rules here. If I don't have one of the items, I simply substitute something else. I also add capers to this recipe. I haven't included capers in the ingredients list because it isn't something everyone has on hand. Also capers can be quite pricey. But keep them in mind and if you come across a good deal on them or happen to have some, just add a handful to the mix. It's really wonderful.

Keeping cut apples from going brown:

No one likes cut apples that go brown. To keep apples from going brown, once the apples are diced add them to a bowl, take a bit of lemon juice, just a capful, drizzle it over the apples. Toss the mixture just a bit. Add to your salad. No more brown apples.

Another trick with raisins:

Raisins can be a little chewy and hard, a good way to plump them up a bit is to add them to a small pot. Add a bit of water and a capful of lemon juice. Put the pot on the stove on a very low heat. Give it about 5 minutes then remove the heat and add cold tap water. This restores the raisins a bit and makes them nice and juicy. Once cool add to your salad.

Chicken tacos

1 portion shredded chicken

½ bell pepper

1 small onion

1-2 jalapeno peppers seeded and rind removed (optional, not for the faint of heart)

½ 28 oz can of diced tomatoes

6-8 corn tortillas

2 c shredded lettuce

½ c cheese shreds

Add one portion of the shredded chicken to a microwave safe bowl, chop up bell pepper, onion and add to the chicken. If you like, seed and remove the rind of a couple of jalapeno peppers and chop finely. This is an optional step and if you decide to do it, don't touch your eyes or wipe your nose when dealing with a jalapeno. I would even recommend using rubber gloves and discarding them after. Open the can of diced tomatoes and drain them. We'll only use half the can for this recipe and the other half for another recipe later so store the other half. Take about three tablespoons of the diced tomatoes and add it to the bowl. Sprinkle some adobo to season and stir to mix. Place the bowl in the microwave for 2-3 minutes on medium setting, you just want to heat it not cook it. While the chicken is in the microwave, heat your tortillas on a griddle or frying pan if you don't have a griddle. A couple seconds on each side so they are warm to the touch and flexible. You should prepare about 6-8 tortillas for the same amount of tacos. Once the tortillas & chicken are complete serve with lettuce shreds, the remainder of the tomatoes and cheese.

Chicken enchiladas

1 portion shredded chicken

½ bell pepper

1 small onion

1-2 jalapeno peppers seeded and rind removed (optional, not for the faint of heart)

½ 28 oz can of diced tomatoes

1 can enchilada sauce

12 corn tortillas

½ c cheese shreds

Take a portion of shredded chicken and place in a medium bowl. If you used a large can of diced tomatoes for the tacos and saved the half a can, add the remainder of the diced tomatoes to the bowl. Chop up bell pepper and onion and add them to the bowl and mix well. Open a can of enchilada sauce and pour it in a separate bowl. Heat tortillas on a griddle till softened. Dip a tortilla halfway in the enchilada sauce and place it in a baking dish and fill it with the chicken mixture. Roll the tortilla to resemble a tube with the chicken filling. Be sure to roll the tortilla so the seam faces down. Repeat the process until you've used all the filling. You should have approximately 12. Cover the enchiladas with the remainder of the enchilada sauce. Sprinkle the dish with shredded cheese and bake 10 min until the cheese is melted.

Sunday Dinner

Do people still do Sunday dinner? I don't know but if they don't, bring it back for your family. I can't imagine a better start to a new week than a nice Sunday dinner with friends and family. But what do you serve when money is tight and you want a special meal. With a little planning we can make a special meal with very little. Choose wisely when shopping. In the meat department look for something close to the sell by date and ask for a discount from the in store staff. They want to sell it and you want to cook it, chances are you can strike a deal, if not, you haven't lost a thing.

Here's an easy favorite, Herb Lemon Roasted Chicken, now you want to get a roaster chicken, but if you can't find one or it's too expensive, get a fryer, it's not impossible to make it work.

Herb Lemon Roasted Chicken

1 Roaster chicken

1 lemon

½ package poultry herbs fresh not dry

2 potatoes

2 carrots

Rinse and pat dry the chicken. Place the chicken in a roasting pan. Take a lemon and score it slightly and place the lemon in the cavity of the chicken. Get poultry herbs sold in the vegetable section of the super market. Fresh not dried herbs, as dried herbs are pretty worthless. Chop the herbs finely and sprinkle over the chicken and in the cavity.

Peel and chop the carrots and potatoes into bite size pieces. Add the carrots and potatoes to the roasting pan. Cover the pan and place the pan in a 425 degree oven for about an hour depending on the weight of the bird. Some roaster chickens come with a pop-up timer which is very helpful but the best way to ensure the chicken is done is to use a thermometer in the thickest part of the bird. Temperature should reach 165 degrees to ensure it's fully cooked.

Once the bird is done, let it rest about 20 minutes. This will ensure the bird is not dry. Don't worry about the bird getting cold, it will be warm, moist and delicious.

Homemade Chicken Gravy

½ c Roasted chicken drippings

2 tbsp flour

½ c warm water

While you're resting the chicken, take the drippings from the bird and make a nice homemade gravy. Now the trick to gravy without lumps is premixing the flour in warm water and whisking the mixture before adding to the drippings.

Take ½ cup of the chicken drippings from the roasting pan and place it in a small pot. Turn the burner on low. While the drippings are warming up, take a measuring cup and fill it with ½ cup of lukewarm tap water. Add two tablespoons of flour to this mixture and whisk right in the measuring cup ensuring all the flour is fully incorporated in the water. It should look like milk.

Next add to the drippings slowly whisking the drippings as you pour the flour/water mixture in. As the gravy starts to thicken, make sure your heat is not too high. Gravy should not boil, it should be just simmering. Once properly thickened serve with your rested bird and enjoy.

Chicken dinner leftovers

Your chicken dinner may or may not have leftovers, but even if you only have bones left over, save them. With many of the recipes in this book I've asked you to save juices, drippings and so on. The reason for this is you will be able to make one amazing chicken stock that you will be able to use for gravies, sauces and yes Soup. While you should have chicken soup base on hand, the goal should be to have your own stock ready and waiting whenever the recipe calls for it. Sometimes that won't be possible so use the soup base but whenever you can, use your own stock.

Stuffed Cabbage or Bell Peppers

This recipe holds many memories for me. It's still one of my all-time favorites although I've modified the recipe a good deal over the years. The original used only ground beef and rice mixed with egg. My version has ground turkey and turkey sausage and no rice and no egg. The sauce was a simple tomato sauce and now I use crushed or diced or both. There's a few more steps to my version which I think have improved the taste but that's not to say my mother's weren't the best ever. Just mine are slightly (only slightly) healthier.

This is definitely a weekend meal. There's a bit of prep time to it so I say get the kids to help. This is another family project meal which should be a fun time for all.

The filling for both the cabbage and the peppers is the same, so hence I've bundled both recipes together for you and I hope you cherish this recipe as much as I do.

Filling:

1 package (¼ lbs) ground turkey

1 tube turkey sausage

Garlic salt & pepper to taste

1 28 oz can of crushed tomatoes

Mix together ground turkey and turkey sausage garlic salt and pepper. Open the can of crushed tomatoes and add two tablespoons to the mix. Mix together with your hands (or the kids hands) till combined.

That's your filling, now for the wrapping.

Cabbage – I've changed the recipe from just regular cabbage to savoy cabbage because it's more flexible. But honestly it doesn't matter. Both are equally delicious and if it makes more sense to do regular cabbage, do so with my blessing.

Preparing the cabbage:

Start a large pot of water with a little chicken soup base or your chicken stock if you've made it. Start the heat at medium-high. We want the water to start boiling while we work with the cabbage.

Turn the cabbage upside down to reveal the base. Remove as much of the stalk as you can with a paring knife in order to more easily remove the leaves. Once you've got about a half dozen leaves, slide each of them into the boiling water to wilt them and get them flexible enough for wrapping the filling. They should be in the water no more than 5 minutes. Once they are done, remove them from the water and into a bowl of cold water, preferably with ice. Repeat the same with another 6 leaves.

While the second batch of 6 is in the water, you can begin to start wrapping the filling in the first batch, and place them in a bowl.

Once you remove the second batch of leaves from the boiling water. Turn off the burner and fill the second batch of leaves. You should have a total of 12 stuffed cabbage rolls. Once you do, carefully place the cabbage rolls back in the water you used for wilting the cabbage leaves. Turn the burner back on to low heat setting and let the cabbage simmer for about 15 to 20 minutes. When the cabbage leaves begin to be transparent is when the rolls are complete. Drain the water from the pot. (don't save this water) Add the remainder for the crushed tomatoes and serve.

Preparing the peppers:

8 bell peppers any color should be large

You'll be happy to know there's a lot less work involved in preparing the peppers vs. the cabbage, but this takes a bit more cooking time and needs to be watched carefully to prevent scorching.

First slice the top off the peppers and discard. Clean out the seeds and rind carefully then rinse the peppers under cold water. Fill each of the peppers with the filling and place in a large soup pot or dutch oven. Place the peppers so they support each other and stand upright. Fill the pot with water just enough so most of the pepper is submerged but not so much that the water reaches the filling. Turn the heat on low and let cook for 25-30 minutes. Check the pot regularly to ensure it has enough water and isn't burning. While the peppers are cooking, take the remainder of the crushed tomatoes and pour it into a microwave safe bowl heat on a low setting for 2-3 minutes. Check your peppers by sticking a knife in through the center of one of the peppers. If your knife slides in easily, and the meat shows red juice, it needs a bit longer. If your knife meets a little resistance, your peppers are done. Remove the peppers carefully and plate them. Cover with the remainder of your crushed tomatoes and serve.

Some people serve stuffed peppers with cheese on top. I personally think this is a crime, but to each his own. If you feel these need cheese, go for it, just please don't tell me about it.

Salmon Patties

This is one of my all-time favorite dishes. The only reason I don't cook it more often is because of the bones in canned salmon. It's really a pity they don't remove the bones in canned salmon. I know that you can get the salmon packages that don't have bones, but that's not enough salmon for patties and rather cost prohibitive. The packets are great for salmon salad though.

This is another one of those kid-friendly recipes. Have them dig in and get their hands dirty. When I was a kid, I was strictly against fish. You could not get me to eat fish. This recipe and the tuna noodle minus the casserole were the exception. My mother made them with those fries I told you about earlier. Talk about heaven on a plate, it was absolutely fantastic. Nowadays, if I make salmon patties, I make it without the bread crumbs and I use egg beaters instead of eggs. I also use very little oil. It makes the process pretty challenging. The bread crumbs serve as binding agent so if you're not careful you just end up with salmon bits instead of patties. So for this book I'm sharing the original recipe which will be much easier and less frustrating. But if you like a challenge, just remove the bread crumbs, go down to one egg (egg beaters are $$$) and use a couple of tablespoons of olive or your saved oil. Cook these patties low and slow. If you don't you just end up with crumbly, burnt patties.

Ingredients;

1 can (16 ounces) salmon

1 small onion

Garlic salt & pepper, to taste

2 large eggs

1 c Italian bread crumbs

3 tablespoons of olive or saved oil

Empty the can of salmon into a mixing bowl. Reach in and look for any bones. You can try to find them all with a fork, but I find your hands are much better at finding them. Discard the any bones you find. Chop the onion finely and add to salmon. Season with the garlic salt and pepper. Add the two eggs and mix well with the salmon. Add the bread crumbs and shape into small patties. These should be the size of a lid of a mason jar. You should get about 8 patties. In a skillet over low heat, add the oil and gradually add patties. It's critical that you fry the patties slowly on one side and then the other. They should have a nice brown crust on both sides. Plate and serve. I really encourage you to serve with the best fries ever recipe.

Homemade Chicken stock

Leftovers of Herb Lemon Roasted Chicken

1 large onion, quartered

2 carrots, peeled

2 ribs celery

1 leek, white part only, chopped (this is optional but I encourage you to get it if you can)

Remainder of poultry herbs used in Herb Lemon Roasted Chicken Dinner

1 bay leaf

2 whole cloves garlic, peeled

Juices and drippings saved from Chicken dinner, chicken breast cooking, pasta water*

2 qt Water

Okay, time to get out the stock pot again. Place the chicken in the pot, chop the onion, carrots, leek and celery into good size bites and add to the pot. Chop up the herbs and mince the garlic and add the bay leaf to the pot.

Next add your juices and drippings. *If you don't have all the juices and drippings just use what you have from the Herb Lemon Chicken and a tablespoon of chicken soup base.

Add enough water to cover all the solids and simmer for about an hour. Remember low and slow. Keep your heat low and take your time. We want every bit of flavor we can get. This is a good slow cooker recipe, but I hate slow cookers. Go ahead and do it on the stove. After about an hour you should have a good stock going. Skim the fat off the top as it produces and add to your saved grease. Add more water and simmer another 90 minutes. After 90 minutes, get another stock pot and put your colander in it. Take your stock and pour it into the new pot. Take the strainer out to remove the solids. You should have about two quarts of stock.

Discard the bones from the solids and store the vegetables in a container for later use. Put the stock in its own container and store that in the fridge or freezer for later use.

Chicken Noodle Soup

Now that you have your good chicken stock, let's put it to work on that old standby, chicken noodle soup. What says love better than homemade chicken soup? It's warming and comforting and just delightful.

With this recipe, you've actually got very little to do. You built most of the soup already when you made your stock.

Ingredients:

Vegetables and chicken from making stock

1 qt of chicken stock

½ package of egg noodles

Additional canned vegetables like: green beans, peas and zucchini

First begin a pot of water to boil your egg noodles. I always boil pasta in water with some chicken base added for flavor, but you don't need to do it for this recipe as the noodles will be in your soup.

While the water for your egg noodles is boiling, in another pot pour the chicken stock. Set the heat at medium-high to bring the soup to a boil then reduce to a simmer. Add your vegetables and chicken to the broth.

By now, the water for your noodles has probably come to a boil. Add the noodles and cook to almost al dente then, drain the excess water and set aside.

Return to your stock and add the additional vegetables. Then add your egg noodles and raise the temperature on the stock to medium high again till you get a boil then reduce to a simmer. Let simmer about 5 minutes then serve and enjoy.

When in doubt, have a salad

Salads tend to get a bum rap in our world. They're boring, diet food, not filling and not satisfying at all. They are also perishable so we tend not to make them because it's a lot of work with not a lot reward and then it goes bad before you eat it all.

I get that, but I also think you can make a salad worthy of dinner and make it very satisfying. What's more, you will see this salad go faster than summer in Chicago.

This is my standby salad, which is an unfortunate name, really, because it should be the star of the show. I make a big bowl of it and store in the fridge for the week. Anytime I'm peckish or don't feel like making anything for dinner, I reach for the salad. It's the perfect weeknight meal when served with one of the chicken breasts from the magic chicken breast bag. Serve it with tuna, salmon, chopped up turkey breast or just by itself. Your family will enjoy it.

Standby Salad

1-2 heads of romaine lettuce

½ a bag of baby spinach

1-2 green onions or scallions

½ shallot

Few sprigs of fresh cilantro

Few sprigs of fresh parsley

2 stalks of celery

½ bell pepper

¼ c raisins

1/3 c craisins

1 diced apple

Get out your cutting board and a good knife; there's lots of chopping in this recipe. You'll also need a big salad bowl with a lid. Begin by chopping the romaine lettuce into small bite size pieces and add the lettuce to the bowl. Next repeat the process with the spinach, green onions, shallot, herbs, celery and bell pepper.

Next take the craisins and raisins and put them in a small pot. Fill it with water just enough to cover the craisins and raisins. Add a teaspoon of lemon juice. Put it on the stove and set the heat to low. Let it simmer for about 5 minutes or until you see the water evaporate. Do not let the water evaporate. Remove them from the heat and put them in a small bowl. Add cold tap water to cool and drain it. Now you have nice plump raisins and craisins. Add these to the salad bowl.

Next dice your apple and place it in a bowl with a lid. Add a tablespoon of lemon juice and secure the lid. Now gently shake the container for a couple of seconds. Remove the lid and add the apple to your salad. This prevents the apples from going brown.

Mix all the ingredients well in the bowl. Cover the bowl and place it in your refrigerator until ready to serve.

Adding Chicken:
This is a lovely salad to serve with a protein so here's how you add a chicken breast.

Take one of the chicken breasts from the magic bag of chicken breasts and baste it with a nice lite Italian dressing and a little garlic salt and pepper. Bake or broil it, careful not to overcook it. Once done, slice into strips and serve on top of a bed of standby salad. One of these chicken breasts should serve at least two people once sliced into ¼ inch strips.

Adding Tuna or salmon
Personally, I like to add plain tuna or salmon to this salad with a side of ranch for dipping. It's really very good and I encourage you to try it.

If you want a bit more umph, try this recipe, it the same recipe whether you're using tuna or salmon:

1 can of tuna or tuna sized can of salmon

¼ cup of light ranch dressing

1 teaspoon Dijon mustard (optional, if you don't have it skip it, don't use yellow mustard)

1 stalk of celery

½ shallot finely chopped.

1 hard boiled egg

Mix the first three ingredients well, chop the celery and shallot finely and add to the tuna or salmon. Next peel and chop up the egg and add to the fish. Mix well and serve on a bed of standby salad.

Food for thought

These are very challenging times to raise a family in and you should be applauded for taking the challenge head on. But no one ever said you have to do it all on your own. Reach out to your friends and family and let them know when you need a hand. We can't always help each other monetarily but we can share our knowledge, our compassion, a shoulder to cry on or a meal. I hope you've learned a little something from this modest effort. I thank you for allowing me to share these recipes with you. I wish you and your family all the best and I hope you find down the road that in spite of the struggle, these were the best of times.

Bless you

K

Made in the USA
Las Vegas, NV
29 December 2023

83691512R00039